Remagen Bridge

Remagen Bridge

IAN KEMP

Ian Allan PUBLISHING

Acknowledgements:

Anyone writing about the capture of the Ludendorff Bridge owes a huge debt of gratitude to Ken Hechler. As a US Army historian assigned to the European theater of operations in 1945 Colonel Hechler interviewed many of the participants, both American and German, only months after that the bridge's capture. He continued his research after the war interviewing hundreds of veterans before publishing *The Bridge at Remagen* in 1957. The book is the starting point for anyone interested in the events of those crucial days in March 1945.

As always photographs are an important part of this type of book and I wish to thank Thomas Anderson and Phillip Jarrett for their assistance in supplying images.

I would also like to thank Kurt Kleeman of the Peace Museum at Remagen Bridge and the staff of the Ministry of Defence library. As ever, I also need to thank my wife Helle for her support.

Further reading:

Omar Bradley, *A Soldier's Story*, Holt, New York, 1951.
Peter Chamberlain and Chris Ellis, *British and American Tanks of World War Two*, Cassell, London, 2004.
Peter Chamberlain and Hillary Doyle, *Encyclopedia of German Tanks of World War Two*, Cassell, London, 2004.
Douglas W. Dwyer, *90th Chemical Mortar Battalion, The Story of the Ninetieth In Training and In Action 1944-1945*, US Army Chemical Mortar Battalions Veterans Associations website, 1946.
George Forty, *US Army Handbook 1939-1945*, Sutton Publishing, Stroud, 2003.
Ken Hechler, *The Bridge at Remagen*, Ballantine Books, New York, 2005.
Charles B. MacDonald, *The Last Offensive, The European Theater of Operations, United States Army in World War Two*, Office of the Chief of Military History, United States Army, Washington DC, 1973.
John McGrath, *The Brigade: A History: Its Organization and Employment in the US Army*, Combat Studies Institute, Fort Leavenworth, 2004.
Alfred Price, *Hitler's Jets*, The Elite, Orbis, London, 1986.
Andrew Rawson, *Remagen Bridge*, Leo Cooper, 2004.
Robert S. Rush, *GI The US Infantryman in World War II*, Osprey, Oxford, 2003.
E. Paul Semmens, *The Hammer of Hell, The Coming of Age of Antiaircraft Artillery in WW II*, Air Defense Artillery magazine online, Fort Bliss, 1990.
Nigel Thomas, *The German Army in World War II*, Osprey, Oxford, 2002.
US Army, *The 9th: The Story of the 9th Armored Division*, Stars & Stripes, Paris, 1945.
US Army Corps of Engineers, *Engineer Memoirs - General William M Hoge, US Army*, US Army Corps of Engineers website, Washington DC, 1993.
Russel F. Weighly, *Eisenhower's Lieutenants, The Campaign of France and Germany 1944-1945*, Indiana University Press, Bloomington, 1981.
Steven J. Zaloga, *US Armored Divisions, The European Theater of Operations, 1944-45*, Osprey, Oxford, 2004.
Steven J. Zaloga, *M4 (76mm) Sherman Medium Tank 1943-65*, Osprey, Oxford, 2003.
Steven J. Zaloga, *V-2 Ballistic Missile 1942-52*, Osprey, Oxford, 2003.

TITLE SPREAD: Ludendorff Bridge before the attack. *(Ub)*

Series Created & Edited by Jasper Spencer-Smith.
Design and artwork: Nigel Pell.
Cover design: Crispin Goodall.
Maps: Martin Watts.
Produced by JSS Publishing Limited,
P.O. Box 6031, Bournemouth, Dorset, England.

Photograph Credits
Bob Flemming (RJF),
P. Jarrett (PJ),
Tank Museum, Bovington (TM),
Ullstein bild (Ub),
US Army (US Army)
US National Archives (USNa),
100th Bomb Group Foundation, Michael Faley (101stbg)
303rd Bomber Group Foundation (303rdbg)

First published 2006

ISBN (10) 0 7110 3094 4
ISBN (13) 978 0 7110 3094 7

Published by Ian Allan Publishing

an imprint of Ian Allan Publishing Ltd,
Hersham, Surrey KT12 4RG.
Printed by Ian Allan Printing Ltd,
Hersham, Surrey KT12 4RG.

Code: 0611/B1

visit the Ian Allan Publishing website at:
www.ianallanpublishing.com

CONTENTS

The bridge was a formidable engineering challenge as the Rhine is over 1,148ft (350m) wide at Remagen and has a fast-flowing current.

LUDENDORFF BRIDGE

Following the signing of the Entente Cordiale between Britain and France in 1904 German *Kaiser* Wilhelm II directed *Feldmarschall* Alfred Graf von Schlieffen, Chief of the Imperial General Staff, to develop a plan that would allow Germany to fight a war against both France and Russia. The resulting Schlieffen Plan called for Germany to launch a massive offensive through the Low Countries to defeat France as rapidly as possible and then shift its forces to the eastern front before Russia could complete the mobilisation of its huge army. To do so it was essential that efficient transportation links were built across Germany from west to east. The Rhine was a formidable barrier to an invader planning to attack Germany from the west but it also restricted the movement of German troops. In the years before the outbreak of World War One General Erich Ludendorff worked to ensure the transportation infrastructure, particularly bridges across the Rhine, was in place to implement the Schlieffen Plan. Although the town of Remagen on the west bank of the Rhine was one of three sites identified for a rail bridge, construction did not begin until 1916, by which

LEFT: The view south from the Appollinaris church of the Ludendorff Bridge over the Rhine. The photograph was taken circa 1930. *(JSS)*

time Germany was bogged down in a war on two fronts following the failure of the Schlieffen plan in September 1914. Ironically, Russian prisoners formed part of the labour force which worked round the clock in a two-year effort to complete the bridge.

It was a formidable engineering challenge as the Rhine is more than 1,148.3ft (350m) wide at Remagen, with a fast-flowing current, and the bridge had to be high enough to allow the passage of traffic on the river. Moreover, the east bank is dominated by a steep rocky hill, the Erpeler Ley, which rises 574.15ft (175m) above the level of

the river. A tunnel was dug through the Erpeler Ley while an embankment was built on the west bank of the river to carry the rail line to and from the bridge. The overall length of the bridge was 1,069 feet (326m); three symmetrical arches with spans of 278ft (84.7m), 513ft (156.4m) and 278ft (84.7m) rested on four stone piers. The bridge carried two rail tracks with a footpath on each side and planks could be laid over the rails to allow troops, horses and vehicles to cross. The strategic importance of the bridge was reflected in the security aspects of the design. A pair of heavy stone towers, resembling castle turrets, was

ABOVE: US troops first crossed the Ludendorff Bridge after the Armistice of 11 November 1918. *(USNa)*

built at each end of the bridge to command the local countryside. The towers were three storeys high with gun embrasures at each level and guns could also be mounted on the flat roofs protected by the stone crenellations. There was a passageway connecting each pair of towers enabling the defenders to move between them under complete cover. Collectively the towers had enough space to accommodate an infantry battalion. Two chambers were built in each of the piers that could be packed with hundreds of kilograms of TNT should enemy attack make it necessary to demolish the bridge. Named in honour of Ludendorff, the bridge was formally opened in 1918.

Following the Armistice of 11 November 1918 the III US Corps in December became the first American troops to cross the Rhine when they marched across the Ludendorff Bridge to begin occupation duties in Germany. They were replaced by French troops in 1919. With an eye to the future the French filled the demolition chambers in the bridge piers with cement. As tension between Nazi Germany and France increased German military engineers devised new plans for the demolition of the bridge in 1938. The engineering company Siemens & Schuckert laid an electric-powered fuse cable (encased in a thick steel pipe) connecting 60 demolition charges in zinc-lined boxes, carefully placed to bring the complete bridge crashing into the river. The ignition switch was located in the entrance to the railway tunnel on the east end of the bridge and a circuit tester allowed the electrical circuit to be periodically tested. As a precaution in the event of the electrical ignition failing primer cord could be used to initiate the main charges. The original plan called

ABOVE: An early etching of the Appollinaris church located on the north side of Remagen. *(JSS)*

for explosives to be stored in a shelter close to the bridge until needed.

Reichsführer-SS Heinrich Himmler was responsible for home defence of Germany including the security of the 22 road and 25 railroad bridges across the Rhine. Local control was exercised through the headquarters of the various *Wehrkreise* (Military Districts) into which Germany was divided. In the early years of World War Two a small bridge security company was stationed in Remagen; however, with the deterioration of Germany's fortunes by mid-1943 *Wehrkreis VI* took measures to bolster the protection of the Rhine bridges in its district. *Hauptmann* Karl Friesenhahn was posted with a 180-strong engineer company to the Ludendorff Bridge. He had fought on both the Western and Eastern fronts during World War One as a member of a combat engineer battalion and had

risen to the rank of sergeant before being discharged after being wounded for a third time. Friesenhahn joined the Nazi Party in 1933 and was conscripted in 1939 when Germany invaded Poland, 1 September 1939. Friesenhahn was assigned to an engineer battalion that worked on various Rhine bridges and was commissioned after completing officer candidate school in 1940.

Following the Allied landing in Normandy, 6 June 1944, Hitler still hoped that his forces would be able to repel the invaders before they reached German soil. Nevertheless, half-hearted measures were taken to bolster security along the Rhine which included assigning *Hauptmann* Willi Bratge with his company of the 80th Infantry Replacement & Training Battalion to Remagen on 1 November 1944. Bratge served in the *Reichswehr* from 1923 until 1927, was

commissioned as a reserve lieutenant in 1937 and was mobilised two years later. He participated in both the invasion of Poland and France, where he earned two Iron Cross, and he requested a transfer to the Russian front in 1943. After being seriously wounded in August 1944 Bratge was evacuated to Germany. Like their commander, the men in Bratge's company were soldiers recovering from wounds; in January and February 1945 there was a threefold turnover in the junior ranks as men recovered sufficiently to be posted back to frontline units. By late February Bratge's company, which had numbered approximately 300 when formed in June 1944, had been reduced to 41 men and in early March it numbered only 37. Although Bratge conscientiously planned defensive positions for a regiment his efforts to requisition timber and other essential stores were accorded a low priority, also his men were not suited for heavy labour. Moreover, not a single vehicle was assigned to his unit.

Following the Allied breakout from Normandy the 9th US Air Force began bombing the Rhine bridges in September, the *Luftwaffe* deployed several anti-aircraft units around Remagen. The Ludendorff Bridge was damaged on 19 October 1944 but after two weeks of repairs was reopened to rail traffic. Bombing continued throughout the winter and the viaduct on the left bank suffered extensive damage during a raid on 29 December 1944. By mid-February 1945 there were two platoons equipped with 2cm FlaK guns atop the Erpeler Ley and in Remagen, and a railroad FlaK battalion with two batteries of 2cm and 3.7cm FlaK guns and a heavy battery of 10.5cm guns were in the area. An artillery unit with smoke generators was stationed near the bridge but its effectiveness was dubious as the unit consisted of volunteers recruited from among Russian prisoners, guarded by approximately 20 German soldiers. Air defences were bolstered by deployment of the 3/900th FlaK Training & Test Battery, commanded by *Oberleutnant* Karl Peters, equipped with experimental *Föhngeräte* rocket launchers. At the end of the month the railroad FlaK unit was withdrawn and to Bratge's dissatisfaction the air defence of the bridge was then controlled from a *Luftwaffe* headquarters 6 miles (9.66km) away.

As the Allies approached the Rhine the command of German forces along the river

ABOVE: German artillery equipped with a sIG33 infantry assault fieldgun fire on US forces around Remagen. *(AN)*

ABOVE: The mobile 3.7cm Flak gun was used to great effect as an anti-tank weapon against light tanks and other armoured vehicles. *(Ub)*

became increasingly confused. In February 1945 responsibility for the Ludendorff Bridge was transferred from *Wehrkreis VI* to *Wehrkreis XII.* As *Feldheer* (Field Army) units were forced back the various *Wehrkreis* headquarters were supposed to relinquish authority for the Rhine bridges to the appropriate *Feldheer* commanders. General Janowski, the chief engineer officer in *Generalfeldmarschall* Walter Model's Army Group B headquarters, had been developing plans since September 1944 to protect the bridges and ferries in his sector. Although the LXXIV Corps was falling back toward Bonn and Remagen, Model assigned responsibility for the bridges to *Generalleutnant* Walter Botsch, commander of *Volksgrenadier Division 18*, on 1 March 1945 and instructed him to report directly to General Gustav von Zangen's Fifteenth Army. Botsch worked hard to develop a knowledge of the local situation and advised Model that a division would be needed to defend west of Bonn and that a reinforced regiment was needed at Remagen. On 5 March, Botsch made his third visit to Remagen and conferred with Bratge, Friesenhahn and the commander of the local *Volkssturm* (People's

Storm) militia. Wooden planks were being laid across the rails on the bridge to aid the withdrawal of German units and the officers understood that every soldier, gun and vehicle that could be saved was vital to the defence of the Fatherland. Botsch reviewed the circumstances and arrangements for the demolition of the bridge and Friesenhahn expressed his concern that the explosives he had requisitioned had not arrived. After the bridge at Cologne-Mulheim was destroyed accidentally when an Allied bomb detonated the demolition charges the German high command had directed that demolition charges should be placed on the Rhine bridges only when the enemy was 5 miles (8km) away. To further allay Hitler's concerns explosives were now stored at a distant from the bridges. Acknowledging that Bratge could not possibly defend the bridge with the few troops available Botsch promised to ask for two infantry battalions and supporting units. That evening Botsch briefed Model by telephone on the preparations to defend Bonn, which both commanders believed was the US Army's immediate objective, and also stressed the need for reinforcements at Remagen. With no army troops

On the alert. A 2cm Flak gun crew prepares for action. At left the soldier is using a hand-held rangefinder *(AN)*

ABOVE: The 2cm Flak gun was also used successfully against light armoured vehicles and infantry. *(Ub)*

RIGHT: Men of the *Luftwaffe* man a 2cm Flak gun. *(AN)*

to spare Model promised to ask for an additional *Luftwaffe* battalion to be transferred to Remagen and directed that *Luftwaffe* units already in the area should be used in the infantry role.

The following day Model ordered Botsch to take his headquarters staff and immediately assume command of the LIII Corps. Model told Botsch he had no time to brief his successor, *Generalmajor* Richard von Bothmer. When Fifteenth Army commander Zangen learned of the change he ordered LXVII Corps commander General Otto Hitzfeld to send an officer to assess the situation at Remagen. At 01.00 on 7 March, Zangen ordered Hitzfeld to launch a counter attack with his corps and also gave him responsibility for the Ludendorff Bridge. Zangen's three badly battered corps were facing US forces along a thinly held line approximately 20 miles (32 km) west of the Rhine. Short of vehicles, ammunition and fuel, the general knew a counterattack, if it could be launched, would only delay the US Army for a short period and he would soon need the Rhine bridges if he was to withdraw any of his 75,000 troops. Zangen instructed Major Hans Scheller, his adjutant, to take a radio to Remagen, check the preparations for the demolition of the bridge and assemble what forces he could for the defence. At approximately 02.00 Scheller left Zangen's headquarters with eight men in two vehicles. The roads were choked with retreating German units and in the darkness Scheller's vehicle was separated from the vehicle carrying the radio. As his vehicle was running low on fuel Scheller directed the driver to take a detour to a supply installation in search of petrol.

At Remagen, Bratge listened to reports from the remnants of retreating units that US forces were not far behind. To his frustration Bratge could not contact General Botsch's headquarters in Bonn by either telephone or radio to pass on these messages. At around 21.00 on 6 March he dispatched two messengers to Bonn but one returned a few hours later to report that with the roads jammed with disorganised German troops it would be impossible to get through until daylight. Some days later in a US Army prisoner of war camp Bratge met a lieutenant colonel from Bothmer's staff who had been sent on 6 March 1945 to brief the defenders of the Ludendorff Bridge as to the new command arrangements. With no accurate information on how far the US forces had advanced the unfortunate officer was captured en route to Remagen.

RIGHT: An MG42 gun crewed by what appears to be veterans engage US troops on the Remagen side of the Rhine. *(AN)*

BELOW: The Ludendorff Bridge on 15 January 1945. In the foreground is a mobile 2cm FlaK 38 L/55 anti-aircraft gun sited on the Remagen side of the Rhine. *(Ub)*

'I am, therefore, making logistic preparations which will enable me to switch my main effort from the north to the south should this be forced upon me.'
General Dwight Eiesenhower

2

ALLIED PLANS

Following the failure of Operation 'Market Garden', September 1944, Montgomery's audacious plan to use British and US airborne divisions to seize the bridge across the Rhine at Arnhem in the Netherlands (Holland), Eisenhower implemented a broad front strategy involving a methodical advance by Allied forces to close up to the Rhine across the entire front. Writing to the Combined Chiefs of Staff on 20 January 1945 to explain his strategy for crossing the Rhine and carrying the war deep into Germany, General Eisenhower stated: 'It will be realized that a crossing of the Rhine, particularly on the narrow frontages in which such crossings are possible, will be a tactical and engineering operation of the greatest magnitude.'

Terrain analysis clearly indicated that an advance into Germany would be easier across the open North German Plain leading into the country's industrial heartland than in the mountainous region south of the Ruhr. Eisenhower decided that the northern crossing by Montgomery's 21st Army Group would be the Allies' main effort while General Omar Bradley's 12th Army Group and General

LEFT: A Boeing B-17 of the 101st Bomber Group of the 9th US Air Force based at airfields in the UK. After the breakout from Normandy many bridges and other targets were attacked in advance of Allied ground forces moving into Germany. *(101stbg)*

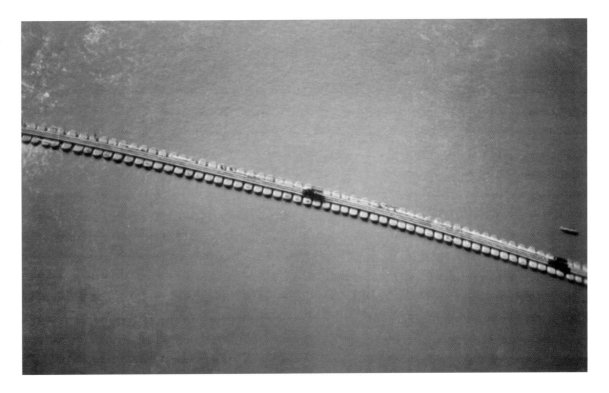

Jacob Dever's 6th Army Group would make secondary crossings in the south. 'The possibility of failure to secure bridgeheads in the north or in the south cannot, however, be overlooked,' warned Eisenhower. 'I am, therefore, making logistic preparations which will enable me to switch my main effort from the north to the south should this be forced upon me.' Eisenhower acknowledged the difficulty of identifying suitable crossing sites in southern Germany, particularly between Cologne and Koblenz: 'there is one site on each side of Cologne suitable for a divisional assault crossing, but a crossing in this area would be tactically difficult, and after the seizure of a bridgehead, the hinterland is unsuitable for the development of operations against opposition.'

The following month planners within Supreme Headquarters Allied Expeditionary Force (SHAEF) were still struggling to select suitable southern crossing sites and subsequent invasion routes. Eventually it was decided that 12th Army Group would cross the Rhine between Mainz and Karlsruhe.

Meanwhile, Montgomery was intensifying his planning for a Rhine crossing that had

LEFT: US infantry supported by M24 Chaffee light tanks, take cover after coming under fire from German forces on the road to Remagen. *(USNa)*

BELOW: Units of the 9th Armored Division assemble in a German village, to make preparations for the attack on Remagen. *(USNa)*

ABOVE: US infantry hitch a ride on an M24 Chaffee light tank. The Chaffee was built by Cadillac and Massey-Harris. It was designed to be a standard chassis for SP guns and special armoured vehicles, the basis of the so named 'Light Combat Team'. *(USNa)*

begun in October 1944 when it was clear that Operation 'Market Garden' had failed. Preparations were on a vast scale, only exceeded by the Allied preparations for the Normandy invasion. The 37,000 engineers of the 21st Army Group would be bolstered by a further 22,000 engineers. More than 3,000 guns were positioned to fire a massive barrage along a 20-mile (32.2km) front to precede the assault while the 17th US Airborne Division and the British 6th Airborne Division prepared to land on the east bank of the river. Having reached the west bank of the Rhine on 9-10 March after closing the Wesel pocket Montgomery selected the night of 23/24 March 1945 as D Day.

9th Armored Division

The 9th Armored Division was one of 16 armoured divisions formed by the US Army during World War Two. The division was activated at Fort Riley, Kansas, on 15 July 1942

by redesignating elements of the pre-war 2nd Cavalry Division, one of two of the army's last horse-mounted cavalry formations. The division's original commander, Major General Geoffrey Keyes, was succeeded in October 1942 by Major General John Leonard who led the 9th until the end of the war in Europe. In June 1943 the division moved to the Desert Training Center (Camp Young) in California. In October 1943 the division moved to Camp Polk, Louisiana, where it participated in extensive manoeuvres conducted by the Third Army from November 1943 until January 1944. Assigned to the European Theatre of Operations the division embarked aboard the RMS *Queen Mary* in New York on 26 August 1944. After a brief spell in the UK to be issued with equipment the Division was landed in France during late September 1944.

Posted to the First Army of Lieutenant General Courtney Hodges, the 9th was assigned to the VIII Corps in Luxembourg. Serving as corps reserve the division was split into

After breaking out from the Remagen bridge-head the division pushed through Germany and was in Czechoslovakia when the war ended. The US Army credited the division with 91 combat days. The division suffered 3,845 battle casualties, including 728 killed. The 9th returned to the US in early October 1945 and was deactivated at Camp Patrick Henry, Virginia, on 13 October 1945.

ABOVE: Members of C Company of the 27th Armored Infantry Battalion, 9th Armored Division, advance through Germany. *(US Army)*

LEFT: US mechanised infantry assemble in a German village. *(US Army)*

three parts when the Germans launched the Ardennes offensive on 16 December 1944. Combat Command A held the south shoulder of the bulge until the advance units of Patton's Third Army arrived. The command then redeployed 60 miles (96.6km) at night in freezing weather to the 4th Armored Division's left flank where it participated in heavy fighting before and after the relief of Bastogne. Combat Command B was first to see action, delaying the advance of the 6th Panzer Army at St Vith. Combat Command Reserve, along with the 28th Infantry Division, withstood the brunt of the attack of the 5th Panzer Army, holding and delaying in front of Bastogne until elements of the 10th US Armored Division and the 101st US Airborne Division could get to Bastogne. Encountering the stubbornly resisting division at such widely separated locations the Germans nicknamed the 9th the 'Phantom Division'.

9th Armored Division
(Major General John W. Leonard)
Headquarters Company
Combat Command A (CCA)
(Col Thomas L. Harrold)
Combat Command B (CCB)
 (Brig Gen William M. Hoge)
Combat Command Reserve (CCR)
(Col Walter Burnside)

2nd Tank Battalion
14th Tank Battalion
(Lt Col Leonard E. Engeman)
19th Tank Battalion

27th Armored Infantry Battalion
(Maj Murray Deevers)
52nd Armored Infantry Battalion
(Lt Col William M. Prince)
60th Armored Infantry Battalion
(Lt Col Collins)

89th Cavalry Reconnaissance Squadron (Mechanized)

3rd Armored Field Artillery Battalion
16th Armored Field Artillery Battalion
73rd Armored Field Artillery Battalion

9th Armored Engineer Battalion
149th Armored Signal Company

131st Ordnance Maintenance Battalion
2nd Armored Medical Battalion
Military Police Platoon
Band

The January 1944 Armored Division Manual (FM 17-100) stated: 'The Armored division is organised primarily to perform missions that require great mobility and firepower.'

The army experimented with different structures for the new armoured divisions before adopting the light armour division Table of Organisation & Equipment on 15 September 1943. The division's primary manoeuvre units were three tank battalions, each of one light and three medium tank companies, and three armoured infantry battalions. Supporting units included three 18-gun artillery battalions, a cavalry reconnaissance squadron of battalion strength, an engineer battalion and divisional services. Instead of brigade or regimental headquarters the division had three combat command headquarters: Combat Command A (CCA), B (CCB) and Reserve (CCR). The division was commanded by a major general, CCA by a brigadier general who was also assistant division commander and the two other combat commands were commanded by colonels. The combat commands had no forces permanently assigned but were intended to be organised for specific missions. Typically a tank battalion, an armoured infantry battalion and an artillery battalion were assigned to each command from which the commander would organise two task forces. One task force would consist of one tank and two infantry companies under the command of the infantry battalion commander and the other would consist of one infantry and

ABOVE: US Army Light Tank M5A1 advancing through a German town in 1945; the commander is ready with the turret machine gun in case of attack. *(TA)*

two tank companies under the tank battalion commander. In practice the combat commands often became permanent groupings. Instead of forming new divisions the army made every effort to keep the existing divisions up to strength.

Made up largely of former horse cavalrymen of the famous 2nd Cavalry Division, the 9th was activated 15 July, 1942, at Fort Riley (Camp Funston), Kansas. One unit, the 3rd Armored Field Battalion, has a battle record dating back to 1794. The battalion fought in every major military campaign in American history.

The 9th trained for nearly a year at the Fort Riley reservation, then went to the Mojave desert near Needles, California, for additional hardening. Reorganized as a light armored division, the 9th participated in Louisiana manoeuvers where its army commander was General Hodges.

The 9th was well known before entering combat. The division had carried out two firing demonstrations in the spring of 1944 while stationed at Camp Polk, Louisiana. The first was for the US press and radio representatives; the second for the press of Allied and neutral nations.

A light armoured division such as the 9th included 77 M5 light tanks, 168 M4 medium tanks, 18 M4 105mm assault guns, 54 M7 105mm SP artillery pieces, 54 M20 armored cars, 450 M3 halftracks, 1,031 motor vehicles, and eight light observation aircraft. Total personnel strength was 10,754.

Lieutenant General John Leonard (1890-1974)

John William Leonard graduated from West Point in the famous class of 1915, 'the class on which the stars fell', and was assigned to the 6th Infantry Regiment. His first active service was with Pershing's punitive expedition into Mexico in 1916. During World War One he fought as a battalion commander in the St Mihiel Salient and in the Meuse-Argonne offensive where he earned a Distinguished Service Cross. After the war the army's tanks were assigned to the infantry and Leonard commanded the 15th Tank Battalion in the early 1920s.

Following the outbreak of war in Europe in 1939 the US Army accelerated the development of its armoured force. In 1941 Leonard was given command of the 6th Infantry in the new 1st Armored Division. Later promoted to brigadier general he was transferred to the 4th Armored Division. Major General Leonard assumed command of the recently formed 9th Armored Division in October 1942 and remained in command until the war ended. He inculcated an aggressive leadership style in his commanders during training, telling them: 'Doing nothing in the face of a problem on maneuvers teaches you nothing. Be positive. Remember, in combat the other side is as confused as you are. Doing something keeps the initiative.' During the Battle of the Bulge General Patton was impressed with how well the division's three combat commands were able to fight separated from their divisional commander and asked to have the division assigned to his Third Army. Leonard was awarded the Silver Star for his actions at Remagen on 8 March 1945. The citation stated: 'At great personal risk, he walked fearlessly among the men who had frozen in their positions under shell fire and strafing, urging them to proceed across the river.' In June 1945 Patton told Leonard that he considered him one of the two best tank commanders who had ever served with him and shortly after this Leonard was selected to command the 20th Armored Division.

General William M Hoge (1894 - 1979)

William M. Hoge graduated from the US Military Academy at West Point in the class of 1916. He was commissioned into the Corps of Engineers and commanded a company in the 7th Engineer Regiment at Fort Leavenworth, Kansas in 1917-18. During World War One he won the Silver Star as a company commander during the St Mihiel offensive and was awarded the Distinguished Service Cross for his actions as a battalion commander directing a bridging operation during the Meuse-Argonne offensive in October-November 1918. During the interwar years he taught at the Infantry School at Fort Benning where he met future generals George Marshall and Omar Bradley and commanded an engineer regiment in the Philippines where he met Generals Douglas MacArthur and Dwight D. Eisenhower. In 1942-43 Hoge commanded the troops that built the 1,523 mile (2,451km) ALCAN highway from Dawson Creek, British Columbia to Fairbanks, Alaska to facilitate the defence of Alaska against the threat of Japanese invasion. Hoge was assigned to the Armored Force at Fort Knox, Kentucky in October 1942 and the following month assumed command of Combat Command B, 9th Armored Division, under Major General John Leonard, a friend from World War One. Hoge was posted to England in 1943 to prepare US engineers for the invasion of Europe and subsequently commanded the Provisional Engineer Special Brigade Group at Omaha Beach on D-Day. He was assigned to the 9th Armored Division in November 1944 and directed Combat Command B's stubborn defence of St Vith that helped halt the German offensive in the Ardennes the following month. After Remagen Hoge was assigned to command the 4th Armored Division. After commanding the IX US corps during the Korean war Hoge served as Commander-in-Chief US Army Europe before retiring from the army as a four-star general in January 1955.

Medium Tank M4A3 (76mm) Sherman

In 1940 the US Army launched development of what became the most widely employed Allied tank of the World War Two, the Medium Tank M4 Sherman. Although inferior to German tanks in both firepower and protection the Sherman was rugged, reliable, fast, simple to maintain and easy to build. The M4 first went into action with the British 8th Army at El Alamein in October 1942. The Sherman was originally armed with a 75mm gun but the US Army and British quickly learned that the gun was incapable of defeating German Panther tanks from the front. Although the US Army Ordnance Department had begun work on a 76mm gun in 1942 army officials were divided over the need for the weapon as the 75mm gun was better for firing high explosive rounds in support of infantry. During the war US tanks on average fired 70% high explosive, 20% armour piercing and 10% smoke rounds. Production of 76mm-armed Shermans began in January 1944 and these represented approximately 25% of the more than 40,000 M4s built between 1942 and 1946. When the 9th Armored Division arrived in the European Theatre of Operations (ETO) in September 1944 it was almost entirely equipped with the M4A3 (76mm) Sherman. However, even shells from the 76mm gun had difficulty penetrating the frontal armour of a Panther or Tiger tank beyond a range of a few hundred yards. A high-velocity armour-piercing round with a tungsten core offered better penetration but fewer than 20,000 rounds had reached the ETO by early March 1945.

The 9th's tank losses during the Battle of Bulge and the advance into Germany

were replaced by whatever tanks were available so that by early March the division had a mixed fleet of 75mm and 76mm gunned Shermans.

Crew:	commander, driver, assistant driver, gunner, loader
Battle weight:	70,000 – 72,800 lb (35,752 – 33,022kg)
Length:	24ft 3in (7.39m)
Width:	8ft 9½in (2.68m)
Height:	9ft 9in (2.97m)
Armament:	one 76mm M3 gun one .50 calibre Browning MG one .30 calibre Browning MG

Ammunition stowage:
71 rounds of 76mm
6,250 rounds of .30 calibre

Minimum armour thickness:
47 in (12mm)

Maximum armour thickness:
2.44 in (62mm)

Maximum road speed:
29mph (437kph)

Maximum cross-country speed:
20mph (32kph)

ABOVE:
Heaviest of all the Shermans was the 'Jumbo'. Known as the M4A3E2, over 250 were built by Grand Blanc between May and June 1944. These were rushed to Europe where they performed very well. A few were fitted with 76mm guns but most had the standard 75mm. *(TM)*

RIGHT:
A Medium Tank M4A3 Sherman armed with a 76mm Gun M1. *(TM)*

M26 General Pershing Heavy Tank

In 1942 the US Army Ordnance Department began development of a 90mm tank gun in parallel with the development of two improved medium tanks. This work culminated in the production of the Heavy Tank T26E3 in late 1944. In March 1945 the tank was reclassified as the Heavy Tank M26 General Pershing. Following early German success in the Battle of the Bulge the Army General Staff directed that all available T26E3s be shipped to the ETO without further testing. The first 20 tanks arrived in January 1945 and the 3rd and 9th Armored Divisions each received 10. In the 9th Armored Division these were used to form a temporary fourth platoon in two tank companies. The M26 proved to be more mobile than the Tiger and the 90mm gun was almost a match for the German 88mm gun. Between November 1944 and June 1945 1,436 M26s were built.

Crew:	commander, driver, assistant driver, gunner, loader
Battle weight:	92,000 lb (41,731kg)
Length:	28ft 10in (8.8m)
Width:	11ft 6in (3.5m)
Height:	9ft 1in (2.7m)
Armament:	1 x 90mm M3 gun 1 x .50 calibre Browning MG 2 x .30 calibre Browning MG
Ammunition stowage:	70 rounds of 90mm 550 rounds of .50 calibre 5,000 rounds of .30 calibre
Minimum armour thickness:	.51in (13mm)
Maximum armour thickness:	4.02in (102mm)
Maximum road speed:	20mph (32kph)
Maximum cross-country speed:	5.2mph (8.4kph)

ABOVE:
Moving an M26 Pershing across the Rhine on a makeshift pontoon. Note each of the boats is powered by a single outboard motor. *(USNa)*

ABOVE LEFT:
The M26 General Pershing was first used in action in Europe. Later in 1945 M26s were used in the taking of Okinawa. *(USNa)*

RIGHT:
Pershings from the 2nd Armored Division passing the burning Town Hall in Magdeburg, Germany, 1945. *(TM)*

'Do you see that little black strip of
bridge at Remagen? If you happen to get
that your name will go down in glory.'
General Milliken to General Leonard, 6 March 1945

'WE HAVE A BRIDGE INTACT OVER THE RHINE'

On 6 March US III Corps headquarters restricted artillery fire against the Ludendorff Bridge to time-and proximity-fuzed ammunition to minimise damage to the structure and asked First Army headquarters to halt bombing raids at Bonn and Remagen.

Lieutenant General Courtney Hodges' US III Corps consisted of the 1st, 9th and 78th Infantry Divisions and the 9th Armored Division in early March 1945. The corps mission within Bradley's Operation 'Lumberjack' was to advance to the Rhine and swing south to link up with units of Lieutenant General George Patton's Third Army thereby trapping as many German units as possible on the west bank of the river. Spearheading the corps' rapid advance the 9th Armored Division reached the town of Stadt Meckenheim, approximately 10 miles (16km) west of the Rhine, on the evening of 6 March 1945. The division's primary objective for 7 March was to seize the crossings over the Ahr River near where it flowed into the Rhine and thus secure the route south to link up with the Third Army. Colonel Thomas Harrold's CCA was given the task of

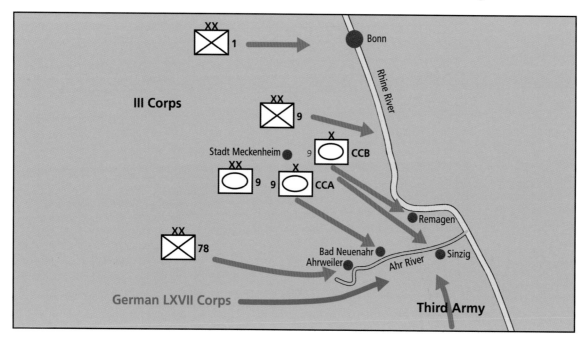

ABOVE: The view of Ludendorff Bridge which greeted Lt. Timmermann and 2nd Lt. Burrows from their vantage point just 1.24 miles (2km) away. *(Ub)*

advancing on the right to cross the Ahr River at Bad Neuenahr to cut the escape of the Germany LXVII Corps along the Ahr Valley. Advancing on the left the primary mission of Brigadier General William Hoge's CCB was to seize the crossing of the Ahr at Sinzig. A secondary mission was to advance to Remagen and then advance along the west bank of the Rhine to Sinzig.

Although Hoge was assigned a tank battalion and two armoured infantry battalions he decided to operate as only two task forces because one of his battalion commanders lacked experience. Lieutenant Colonel (Lt Col) William

Prince, commander of the 52nd Armored Infantry Battalion, was given his own battalion, two of the 14th Tank Battalion's tank companies and an armoured engineer platoon. As the command's main effort he was to advance on the left flank of CCA to the Ahr River and secure bridgeheads at Westum and Sinzig. Lieutenant Colonel Leonard Engeman's task force consisted of the remainder of his 14th Tank Battalion, the 27th Armored Infantry Battalion led by Major Murray Deevers and an armoured engineer platoon. Engeman was ordered to advance on the left of Prince until

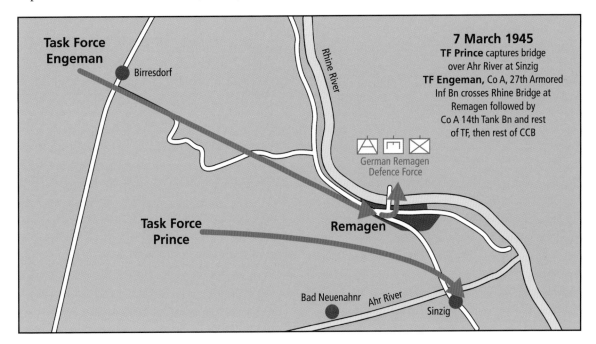

Task Force Engeman

Birresdorf

Rhine River

7 March 1945
TF Prince captures bridge over Ahr River at Sinzig
TF Engeman, Co A, 27th Armored Inf Bn crosses Rhine Bridge at Remagen followed by Co A 14th Tank Bn and rest of TF, then rest of CCB

German Remagen Defence Force

Task Force Prince

Remagen

Bad Neuenahnr   Ahr River

Sinzig

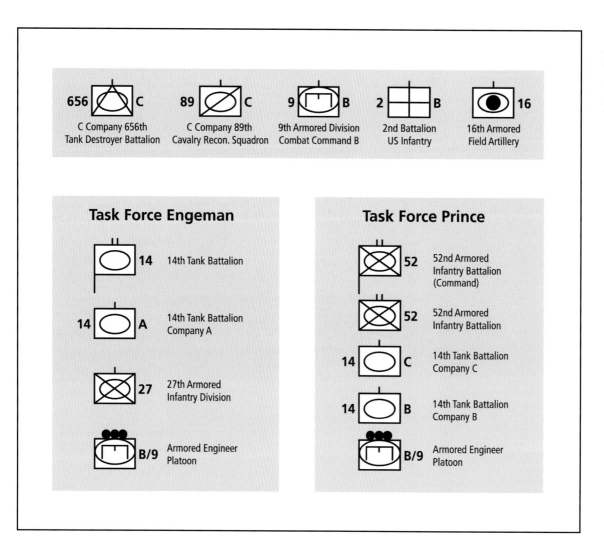

LEFT: The organisation of Combat Command B, 9th Armored Division on 7 March 1945.

he reached Remagen and then advance south along the Rhine. His left flank would be screened by C Troop, 89th Cavalry Reconnaissance Squadron (Mechanized).

Lt Col Leonard Engeman ordered the company commanders of Engeman to assemble at his command post in Stadt Meckenheim at 06.00 on 7 March to receive their orders. 'I just came back from General Hoge and the 'Old Man' wants us to push 10 miles (16km) an hour today,' Engeman began. Issuing specific tasks to his sub units Engeman began with Lieutenant Karl Timmermann who had assumed leadership of the 27th Armored Infantry Battalion's Company A the night before after the previous commander had been wounded after only two days in command. 'Timmermann, you put your doughs (infantrymen) on halftracks and I'll give you a platoon of tanks. You've got an important job to do today. You'll be advance guard for our whole task force'. Captain George Soumas, the commander of A Company, 14th Tank Battalion, was directed to assign his one platoon of M26

Pershing heavy tanks, under Lieutenant John Grimball, to Timmermann's company. The start time, H Hour, was set for 07.00.

The advance got off to a bad start to the frustration of both Hoge and Engeman. Although the division's engineer battalion had worked though the night to clear a route through the rubble in Meckenheim caused by American bombing it was two hours after H Hour before the bulldozers succeeded in opening a passage for Engeman. Finally at 09.00 a platoon of armoured cars from the 89th Reconnaissance Squadron sped off toward Adendorf followed by Timmermann's company. The US forces encountered sporadic fire as they entered Adendorf but were soon mobbed by surrendering Germans. The column brushed aside a lightly defended road block on the east side of the village and continued its advance. Captain Soumas later recalled: 'Throughout the movement, very little opposition was met. The column was constantly being passed by little groups of two or three prisoners marching

ABOVE: Units of the 27th Armored Infantry Battalion, 9th Armored Division, advance through a German town. *(US Army)*

to the rear, hands behind heads, to give themselves up to the nearest authority willing to accept their surrender.'

At 10.30 Hoge received a message that the railway bridge at Remagen was still standing. One of the division's Piper Cub observation aircraft had broken through the low cloud cover over Remagen to find the bridge intact and had immediately radioed the command post of the 16th Armored Field Artillery Battalion with the news. Hoge ordered his operations officer, Major Ben Cothran, to find Engeman and urge him to press on with all speed. Hoge, believing the Germans would blow the bridge before his men arrived, joined Prince to monitor the main effort against the Ahr.

At Remagen on the morning of 7 March 1945 *Hauptmann* Friesenhahn was still waiting for the explosives for the demolition of the Ludendorff Bridge to arrive. Shortly after 11.00 a truck arrived carrying only 300kg (661.4lb) of

commercial Donerit-type explosive instead of 600kg (1,322.75lb) of more powerful military explosives specified in the demolition plan. As the engineer considered how best to distribute the explosives Major Scheller finally arrived at Remagen, still without his radio vehicle. Finding *Hauptmann* Bratge at the traffic control point near the Remagen railroad station Scheller announced that he was the new 'commandant of Remagen'. After a quick conversation the two officers realised the gravity of the situation: instead of two infantry battalions to defend the bridge Scheller learned that the only organised force on the west bank was Bratge's company of less than 40 men under the command of *Feldwebel* Rothe, now deployed in outposts on the Victoriasberg heights overlooking Remagen. The anti-aircraft batteries that were supposed to bolster the west bank defence had already withdrawn across the Rhine. While the two officers were talking a messenger arrived to report that Bratge's men

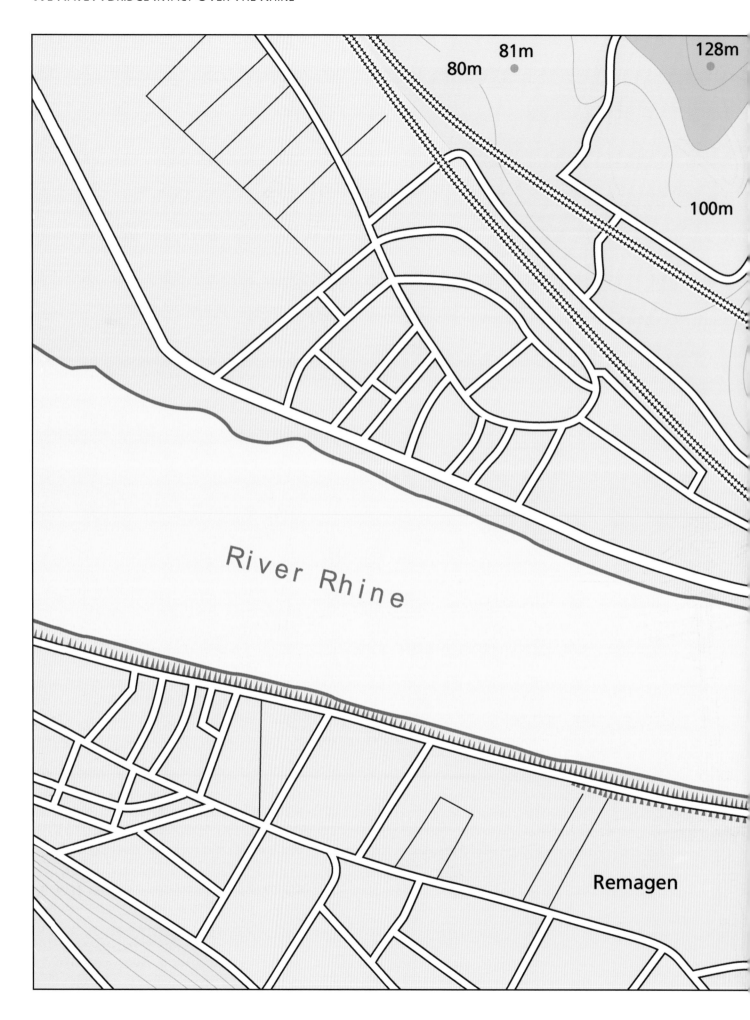

81m
80m
128m
100m

River Rhine

Remagen

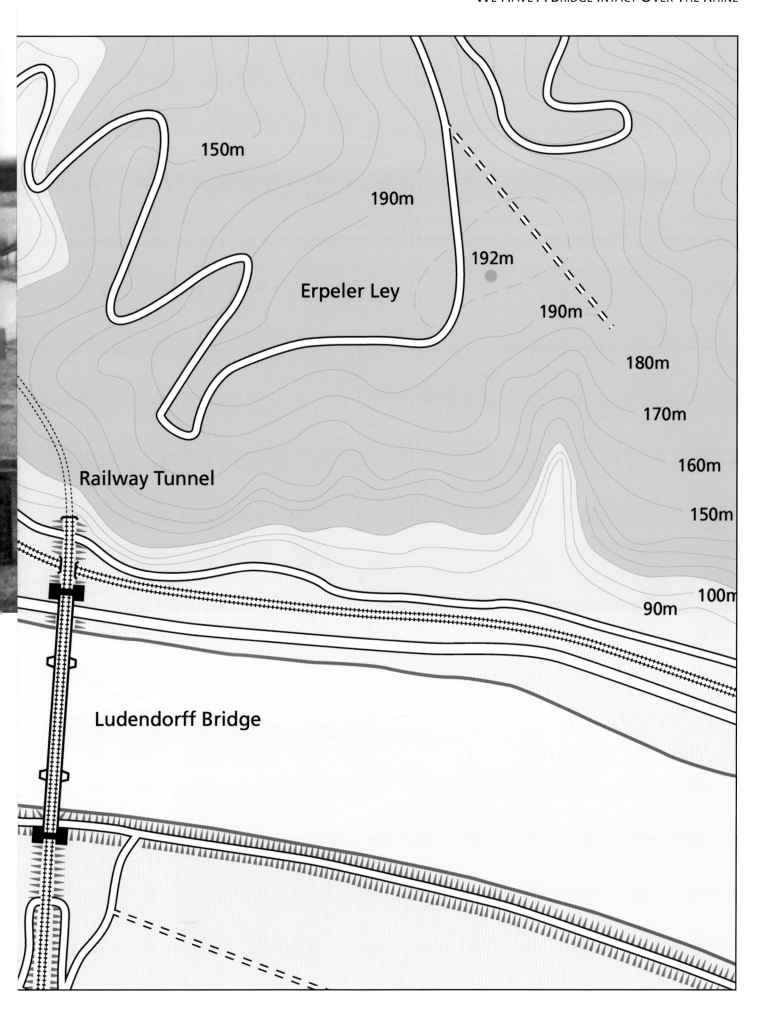

150m

190m

192m

Erpeler Ley

190m

180m

170m

160m

150m

Railway Tunnel

100m

90m

Ludendorff Bridge

LEFT: A US soldier on anti-aircraft duty in one of the many narrow sidestreets of Remagen. The vehicle is a Half-Track Car M3 A1 armed with a .50in M2HB heavy machine gun. A .30in Browning Automatic Rifle (BAR) is at the side of the soldier. *(TA)*

were being attacked by US forces. The two immediately set off to inspect the preparations at the bridge. Scheller instructed Bratge to withdraw his company from the heights to provide close protection at the bridge but Bratge received no response when he tried to relay the instruction over his field telephone. Shortly before 13.00 Scheller ordered Bratge to move the command post from the west bank into the railroad tunnel. Scheller's determination to delay the destruction of the bridge to allow as many retreating troops as possible to cross was reinforced when an artillery officer from *Volksgrenadier-Division 277* arrived to report that his horse-drawn battalion was en route to Remagen bridge. He refused Friesenhahn's request to arm the demolition charges.

As Major Cothran caught up with the tail of Engeman's advance Lieutenant Timmermann's company was moving through the woods on the western slope of the Scheidskopf; on the eastern side, the ridge dropped steeply to the Rhine. Timmermann, the son of German immigrants, had stopped his jeep to talk with occupants of the Waldeschlossen tavern when he was called forward by 2nd Lieutenant Emmett Burrows whose platoon was on point. 'Hey, Tim, take a look that!', cried the excited Burrows. 'Dammit, that's the Rhine,' replied Timmermann, 'I didn't think it was that close.' Both officers watched in astonishment as German troops moved across the bridge less than 1.24 miles (2km) away. Summoned forward, Colonel Engeman and Major Murray Deevers soon arrived at the head of the column. Engeman's first reaction was to call for artillery fire on the troops crossing the bridge but the request was refused by the 16th Armoured Field Artillery Battalion which had been told US forces were near the bridge. The frustrated

Engeman ordered Deevers to develop a plan to capture the town with his infantry while Engeman moved the tanks into positions to provide fire support. Deevers instructed Timmermann and Lieutenant William McMaster, the commander of C Company, to make a reconnaissance into town and locate the best routes to the objective. The two officers led a patrol approximately 440yd (400m) into the town and then returned to report to Deevers that they met no opposition. Deevers instructed Timmermann to take his company on the most direct route through Remagen to the bridge embankment. Grimball was told to start 20 minutes after Timmermann then 'barrel down the hill and go through and cover the bridge with tank fire' followed by C Company mounted in halftracks. Company B would follow Timmermann and complete the clearing of the town. At 14.00 A Company moved into Remagen with Burrows'

platoon in the lead. Although there were no signs of resistance every man was alert for snipers.

As the US forces cautiously moved into Remagen *Hauptmann* Friesenhahn was waiting anxiously with four of his sappers near a charge that had been prepared on the western embankment of the bridge to delay enemy armour. With the bridge already under tank and small arms fire Friesenhahn saw US infantry approaching from the north at around 14.00 and ordered the charge blown. The explosion blew a 30ft (10m) wide crater. As Friesenhahn ran across the bridge with his men he was knocked over by the blast of a tank shell and slipped into unconsciousness. After regaining his senses the winded officer reached the command post in the Erpeler tunnel at 14.45.

Major Cothran emerged from the woods in his jeep and joined Engeman's command group watching the advance into Remagen. 'Don't you

think we ought to bring some artillery fire down on all that?,' asked Engeman pointing toward the Germans moving across the bridge and several trains getting up steam on the east bank. Amazed at seeing the bridge still standing Cothran responded: 'My God, I've got to get the Old Man!'

Moving across country General Hoge arrived about 15.00. He later recalled: 'I got up to the Rhine and stood there on the bank and looked down and there it was. The bridge was there right above the town. I couldn't believe it is true.' He quickly calculated the risks involved in capturing the bridge: it could be blown while troops were crossing with the loss of a platoon or it could be blown after a battalion or more had crossed leaving his men isolated on the enemy bank. He was in no doubt that the prize, a bridge across the Rhine, was worth the gamble.

'I knew it was right,' he recalled in a post-war interview. 'I felt inside me that I could

never live with that knowledge, that I had given up that opportunity without making a try for it. That was probably the greatest turning point in my whole career as a soldier, to capture Remagen.'

His mind made up Hoge said: 'Engemann, Deevers, Russell, get those men moving into town!' Engemann responded that his men were already moving through the town. Hoge was aware that a German prisoner captured by Prince in Sinzig had said the Ludendorff Bridge would be blown at 16.00. 'Engeman was a good man, a good tank commander, but he was very cautious and he wasn't moving fast enough to get down to that bridge. The question was minutes,' recalled Hoge. 'I told him to get them down there now and get going – move!'

The only significant opposition encountered by Burrows' platoon was an automatic weapon firing in the town square. As he moved to outflank the gun two of Gimball's Pershings arrived and fired several 90mm rounds that

Feindhörer u. Gerüchteverbreiter find
Volksverräter, die den Tod ve lienen.

ABOVE: A reconnaissance unit of the 89th Armored Reconnaissance Squadron (Mechanized), 9th Armored Division travelling down Marktstrasse towards the Ludendorff Bridge. The lead jeep is followed by two M-8 armoured cars. The lightly-armoured vehicle type was given the name Greyhound by the British due to its speed. *(USNa)*

silenced the enemy. Realising that resistance was futile *Feldwebel* Rothe and a few men abandoned their position near the Hotel Waldburg and tried to slip past the US troops. Nearing the embankment Rothe came under machine gun fire that forced him to take cover. When the fire halted he resumed running only to be knocked over by a bullet in his leg and although hit a second time by a .50 calibre bullet he managed to drag himself onto the bridge and cross to Erpeler tunnel. Rothe was the last German to cross.

Deevers located Timmermann near the embankment and asked simply: 'Do you think you can get your company across that bridge?'

'Well, we can try it, sir,' Timmermann replied.

'Go ahead,' ordered Deevers.

At about the same time Engeman was briefing Lieutenant Hugh Mott, a platoon leader in B Company, 9th Armored Engineer Battalion. The engineer was told to accompany the infantry onto the bridge, check for demolitions and mines, and determine if the bridge was strong enough to carry tanks.

Although bleeding profusely, Rothe reached the tunnel to report his handful of men had been overrun. By now a smoke screen was building up as Soumas' tanks fired white phosphorous shells at the eastern bank. Confronting Scheller, Bratge said: 'Major, unless you issue the order to demolish the bridge, I shall have the bridge demolished myself.' Realising he could delay no longer Scheller responded: 'Go ahead and have the bridge demolished!' Bratge, instructed his second in command to record that the demolition order was given at 15.20 and then scrambled to Friesenhahn to relay the order. The engineer officer's first response was to demand the order in writing but without waiting further he called out for everyone to take cover and open their mouths, and then moved to the ignition box. Although the circuit had been tested only

minutes before when Friesenhahn wound the key nothing happened. He frantically wound the key a second and a third time before he accepted the grim truth that the circuit was broken. He ordered a repair team to locate the break and repair the circuit but then realised there was no time. Calling his NCOs together he asked for volunteers to ignite the primer cord fixed to an emergency demolition charge which was located on the bridge about 49.7ft (80m) from the tunnel entrance. To his disappointment only one man responded. Braving tank and small arms fire *Feldwebel* Faust darted onto the bridge and ignited the cord.

Karl Timmermann had only just begun to brief his platoon leaders crouched near the railway embankment when the demolition charges exploded. Germans and Americans watched in awe as a huge cloud of smoke and dust boiled around the eastern pier of the bridge and debris showered down. Sergeant Mike Chincar, commanding the 1st Platoon, expressed the thoughts of many men in

A Company: 'Thank God, now we won't have to cross that damned thing!' Their relief was short-lived. As the smoke cleared Timmermann exclaimed: 'Look, she's still standing!' Calling his platoon commanders together Timmermann's orders were terse: 'OK, Jim, Mike and Joe, we'll cross the bridge. Order of march, 1st Platoon, 3rd Platoon and then 2nd Platoon.' 2nd Lieutenant Emmet 'Jim' Burrow, the company's only other officer, was instructed to bring his platoon in the rear to ensure that the attack did not falter. Once across the bridge the lead platoons were to fan out to the left and right while 2nd Platoon was given the daunting task of scaling the Erpeler Ley.

Watching from the heights General Hoge saw the eastern end of the bridge rise up and settle and crash back onto the eastern pier seemingly still intact. 'We still had foot passage across and the bridge was still standing,' recalled Hoge. 'That was when I didn't know what was going to happen. I was waiting for the thing to fall and luckily it didn't do it.'

ABOVE: The crew of a Multiple Gun Motor Carriage M16 on alert whilst other US vehicles cross the bridge. *(JSS)*

RIGHT: M4A3 Sherman medium tanks and infantry cross the Ludendorff Bridge soon after it was captured. *(USNa)*

A 90mm shell fired from Grimball's Pershing cracked one of the bridge towers on the bridge. The muzzle blast knocked Chinchar and some of his men off their feet just as they were starting across the bridge. 'Dammit what's holdin' up the show? Now get goin'!', yelled Timmermann. As tanks, tank destroyers, artillery and mortars fired white phosphorous shells across the river a thick smoke was building up as the 'doughs' of A Company scrambled up the embankment. Chinchar's men cleared the twin towers on the west bank only to find them unoccupied. However, the bridge was swept with fire from machine guns in the eastern towers, snipers and bursts from 2cm FlaK guns that had not yet been silenced by the US forces on the high ground on the western bank. Encouraged by Timmermann and his platoon and squad leaders, the men of A Company leapfrogged across the bridge, seeking shelter behind the beams and railings to provide covering fire for their comrades. After only a few minutes the point platoon

passed the gaping hole in the wooden decking above the eastern pier.

Sergeant Joseph DeLisio, leading the 3rd Platoon, believed that speed was the best way to survive and ran past the towers on the German side. When he realised that fire from the towers had pinned his men down, DeLisio ran back and smashed open the door of the right hand tower. Climbing the spiral staircase he opened a door on the first level where he found three Germans bending over an MG42 machine gun and fired a few rounds as he called on them to surrender. DeLisio heaved the MG42 through the embrasure and pushing the Germans in front of him moved up the stairs next level. A few carbine rounds encouraged an officer and a soldier at the next level to surrender and DeLisio then herded his prisoners onto the bridge and motioned for them to make their own way to the US side. Sergeant Chinchar and two men cleared the other tower, capturing a single German manning a machine gun. Unaware his platoon leader was in the

'The whole Allied force is delighted to cheer the First Army whose speed and boldness have won the race to establish the first bridgehead over the Rhine.'
General Dwight D. Eisenhower

4

A BULL BY THE TAIL

As Colonel Engeman pushed his task force across the bridge General Hoge drove to his command post at Birresdorf to meet his divisional commander. As General Leonard climbed out of his vehicle Hoge said simply: 'Well, we got the bridge.'

'That's a hell of a note,' replied Leonard with wry humour. 'Now we've got a bull by the tail and caused a lot of trouble. But let's push it and then put it up to corps.'

When the news was radioed to III Corps headquarters Colonel James Phillips, the chief of staff, instructed 9th Armored Division to exploit the bridgehead with the troops on hand while he arranged to have the division relieved of its mission to push south. While Phillips contacted General Millikin another staff officer passed the news to First Army headquarters. When General Hodges learned of the crossing shortly after 18.00 he immediately set his staff to work to exploit the opportunity and telephoned General Bradley.

Bradley recalled in his autobiography: 'I was stunned and exhilarated. 'Hot dog, Courtney,' I exclaimed, 'this will bust him wide open. Are you getting stuff across?' Courtney said in his quiet way 'Just as fast as we can push it over.' He

LEFT: Anti-infantry barbed wire defences piled up on the railway embankment. *(US Army)*

ABOVE: US forces cross the bridge from Remagen whilst German prisoners return from Erpeler Ley. *(Ub)*

RIGHT: Ludendorff bridge intact after being captured. *(AN)*

RIGHT: A shell from German artillery explodes near the Remagen side of the bridge. *(US Army)*

had already ordered up US Navy landing craft, which we had stockpiled for a possible Rhine crossing. Army engineers had been summoned forward with pontoon bridges. 'Shove everything you can across it, Courtney,' I said, 'and button up the bridge-head tightly.'

General Harold Bull Supreme, the SHAEF operations officer who was visiting Bradley's headquarters, was not as enthusiastic: 'Sure you've got a bridge, Brad, but what good is it going to do you? You're not going anywhere down there at Remagen. It just doesn't fit into the plan.'

ABOVE: US forces on the Erpeler side of the Rhine before advancing further into Germany. *(US Army)*

LEFT: Military police units from the 9th Infantry Division had the difficult task of keeping traffic moving across the bridge. *(USArmy)*

CROSS THE RHINE WITH DRY FEET
COURTESY OF 9ᵀᴴ ARM'D DIV.

ABOVE: A US Army M3A1 Half Track Car crosses the bridge. *(USNa)*

Bradley acknowledged in his autobiography: 'The terrain opposite Remagen was less than ideal for military manoeuvre. There lay the Westerwald, a dense, mountainous forest, good for defence, poor for offence. We would have to go around the Westerwald. Fortunately, the north-south Ruhr-Frankfurt autobahn lay only 6 miles (9.7km) beyond the Rhine. If Hodges could establish a strong bridgehead opposite Remagen, resist the inevitable counterattack and fight to the autobahn, we could send his troops south on the highway to Limburg, then swing east along the Lahn River Valley to Giessen.'

Annoyed by Bull's continued objections Bradley snapped: 'What the hell do you want us to do, pull back and blow the bridge up?'

The First Army commander telephoned Eisenhower. The Supreme Commander wrote in his autobiography that when Bradley 'reported that we had a permanent bridge across the Rhine I could scarcely believe my ears. He and I had frequently discussed such a development as a remote possibility but never as a well-founded hope. I fairly shouted into the telephone: 'How much have you got in that vicinity that you can throw across the river?'

He said, 'I have more than four divisions but I called you to make sure that pushing them over would not interfere with your plans.'

I replied, 'Well Brad, we expected to have that many divisions tied up around Cologne and now those are free. Go ahead and shove over at least five divisions instantly, and anything else that is necessary to make certain of our hold.'

His answer came over the phone with a distinct tone of glee. 'That's exactly what I wanted to do but the question has been raised here about conflict with your plans and I wanted to check with you.'

According to Bradley, Eisenhower responded, 'To hell with planners.'

The most famous photograph of the Ludendorff Bridge. It was taken from the entrance to the Erpeler Ley tunnel after the capture by US forces. The mouth of the tunnel was sealed after the end of World War Two . *(US Army)*

'An important bridge across the Rhine has fallen into enemy hands without being damaged, despite the fact that all preparations for its demolition had been made'
Generalfeldmarschall Albert Kesselring

5

CONSOLIDATION

Hitler immediately began searching for scapegoats to blame for the loss of the Ludendorff Bridge. He dismissed *Generalfeldmarschall* Gerd von Rundstedt and summoned *Generalfeldmarschall* Albert Kesselring from Italy to replace him. Hitler had previously dismissed Rundstedt in December 1941 and July 1944. *Generalmajor* Richard von Bothmer committed suicide a few days after being sentenced to five years' imprisonment.

Hitler selected *Generalmajor* Rudolf Hübner, an ardent Nazi who was then commanding a *Volksgrenadier* division on the Russian front,

to lead a three-man tribunal to punish those believed responsible for the loss of the bridge. The results were a foregone conclusion. *Hauptmann* Bragte was sentenced to death in absentia. On 13 March 1945 Major Scheller was found guilty of delaying in issuing the order to destroy the bridge and for abandoning his men instead of launching an immediate counter-attack. *Oberleutnant* Karl Peters was found guilty of allowing some of his anti-aircraft battery to fall into enemy hands. Both officers were shot in the back of the neck. The two engineer majors, Kraft and Strobel, despite having organised a

LEFT: The bridge under repair. Note the rail tracks have been boarded over (originally by retreating German forces) to allow vehicle access. *(US Army)*

counterattack with the limited resources at their disposal were also sentenced to death. Inexplicably the tribunal found *Hauptmann* Captain Friesenhahn not guilty and acquitted him in absentia.

Kesselring issued a message stating that 'an important bridge across the Rhine has fallen into enemy hands without being damaged, despite the fact that all preparations for its demolition had been made. This has happened because the responsible leaders have abandoned the bridgehead. They have acted in an irresponsible and cowardly way. The five guilty officers were condemned to death by court martial, one of them a captain, in absentia. The sentence was executed against three majors and one first lieutenant. The above information is to be communicated to all troops as rapidly as possible and should be considered as a warning to everyone. Who does not live in honour will die in shame.'

As news of the capture of the Ludendorff Bridge spread throughout the First Army headquarters staff at all levels quickly took steps to reinforce the bridgehead. The First Army allocated two additional divisions to III Corps to

LEFT: The bridge from the village of Erpeler on the eastern bank of the Rhine. (USNa)

General Janowski, who had arrived earlier that day, supported the view that the engineers should be used to ferry troops across the river. After a heated exchange a compromise was reached. The commander of the 403rd Engineer Training Regiment would use those engineers already en route to Remagen to attack the bridgehead while Strobel continued the ferry operation.

By contrast the US army build up proceeded rapidly and almost 8,000 US troops crossed the bridge in the first 24 hours after its capture. These included the 27th Armored Infantry Battalion, 52nd Armored Infantry Battalion, 14th Tank Battalion, C Company of 656th Tank Destroyer Battalion, C Troop of the 89th Reconnaissance Squadron, a platoon from B Company, 9th Armored Engineer Battalion all of the 9th Armored Division; the 47th Infantry Regiment and 1st Battalion, 60th Infantry Regiment, both of the 9th Infantry Division; the 311th Infantry Regiment and the 1st and 2nd Battalions of the 310th Infantry Regiment of the 78th Infantry Division; and, one and a half batteries of the 482nd Anti-Aircraft

Artillery Automatic Weapons Battalion. Units were fed into the perimeter by Hoge as they arrived. As reinforcements continued to arrive the northern sector of the perimeter was occupied by the 78th Infantry Division, the centre by the 9th Infantry Division and the southern sector by the 99th Infantry Division.

Hitler's insistence that his commanders defend Germany west of the Rhine meant that there were few reserves east of the river to contain the US bridgehead. On the morning of 8 March, Model ordered the 11th Panzer Division at Bonn to abort a planned counter-attack west of the Rhine, cross the river, crush the US forces' toehold at Remagen and destroy the Ludendorff Bridge. On paper a 1944 Panzer Division consisted of 14,727 men organised into a two-battalion tank regiment, the first equipped with PzKpfw IV and the second with PzKpfw V Panther tanks; two two-battalion *Panzergrenadier* regiments with one battalion equipped with half-tracks; an armoured reconnaissance battalion, a self-propelled artillery battalion; a self-propelled anti-tank

RIGHT: An M1
Bofors mobile
anti-aircraft gun
and crew on the
Remagen side of
the Rhine. *(USNa)*

RIGHT: An M1 Bofors mobile anti-aircraft gun and crew on the Remagen side of the Rhine. *(USNa)*

battalion; a motorised anti-aircraft battalion; an armoured engineer battalion; an armoured signals battalion; a field replacement battalion; and, divisional service support units. However, by March 1945 most of these divisions were little more than battle groups short of men, vehicles, ammunition, fuel and spares. The 11th mustered about 4,000 men, 25 tanks and 18 artillery pieces. The division's move was slowed by the need to find scarce petrol, the chaotic situation on the roads and by Allied air attacks. The lead elements did not begin moving until the evening of the 8th and it was not until 10 March that they were in position to attack the US force's perimeter.

Model also appointed *Generalleutnant* Fritz Bayerlein, commander of the veteran Panzer Lehr Division, to command the effort to repulse the US forces. In addition to the 11th Panzer Division Bayerlein was assigned the 300-strong remnant of his own division with 15 tanks; the 900 men, 15 tanks and 12 field guns of the 9th Panzer Division; and the remnant of

the Panzer-Brigade 106, only 100 men and five tanks. Panzer-Brigade 106 was one of 13 such brigades formed in the summer of 1944 from the remnant of divisions that had been decimated on the Russian Front. The nucleus of the brigade were veterans of the *Panzergrenadier-Division Feldherrnhalle* reinforced by new recruits. The brigade, consisting of one Panzer battalion and a *Panzergrenadier* battalion, had been fighting on the Western front since September 1944 and was now only a shadow of its former self. Bayerlein and his LIII Corps headquarters would have only some 10,000 men under their command. On 9 March Model met Bayerlein to discuss his counterattack plan. Bayerlein wanted to attack the centre of the bridgehead at dusk on 10 March but it was already apparent his forces would not be in place in time. Model vetoed the plan and directed Bayerlein to establish a cordon to contain the bridgehead. This set the pattern for the next two weeks – elements of nine German divisions fought tenacious holding actions

ABOVE: A Bay City crane, mounted on an Autocar U8144T 6x6 chassis, being used to lift the 'pilot' section of a pontoon bridge. (USNa)

LEFT: US Army engineers begin the task of assembling a pontoon bridge across the Rhine. The vehicle is a Corbitt 50SD6 mounted with a Coles Crane. (USNa)

ABOVE: A Multiple Gun Motor Carriage (MGMC) M16 stands guard at the Remagen end of the treadway bridge built by US engineers across the Rhine. The vehicle on the bridge is a Diamond T 975A 6x6 truck with an open cab. *(USNa)*

RIGHT: Two US soldiers in a Jeep drive over a pontoon. The vehicle is fitted with snow chains to the tyres adding to the problem of keeping to the narrow carriageway. *(US Army)*

ABOVE: The Panzer Museum's superbly restored PzKpfw V Panther Ausf A *Panzer-befehlswagen* (command tank). *(RJF)*

LEFT: A PzKpfw V Panther in a defensive position on the outskirts of a Rhineland village. *(Ub)*

RIGHT: The same Panther in action. Note the distinctive aerials as fitted to the command tank. *(RJF)*

BELOW: *Panzer-Kampfwagen* (PzKpfw) V Panther Ausf G *Panzerbefehls-wagen* (command tank). *(Ub)*

ABOVE: An MP on duty on the Erpeler side of the Rhine. Two Jeeps and a Dodge 214A (WC56) command and reconnaissance car are visible. *(USNa)*

LEFT: A US Army Multiple Machine Gun Mount M55. This was designed and manufactured by Maxson and mounted four .50 calibre M2 HBTT machine guns each firing at a cyclical rate of 400-500 rounds per minute, proving lethal to low-flying aircraft. *(USNa)*

RIGHT: To prevent mines launched by the Germans from upstream positions striking and destroying pontoon bridges, US engineers constructed barriers of logs across the river. (USNa)

but were never concentrated in sufficient strength anywhere on the steadily expanding perimeter to mount more than local counter-attacks. When the skies were clear German efforts were severely hampered by the 9th US Air Force which concentrated its efforts on cutting the roads and rail lines leading toward the bridgehead.

The most effective German response was artillery fire. Throughout 8 and 9 March German artillery fired an average of one shell every minute, however shortage of ammunition reduced this rate to only four or five rounds per hour by 10 March. An estimated 50 10.5cm, 50 15cm, three 17cm and at least six 21cm weapons, primarily from PzArtRgt 119 and VolksArtKorps 388, were eventually concentrated around the bridgehead. The war diary of the *Oberkommando der Wehrmacht* (OKW) indicates that the 54cm Mörser (Gerät 041) siege mortar was used to fire 11 massive 4,400lb (1,996kg) shells toward the bridgehead on 20 March; however, the weapon malfunctioned and was withdrawn.

US Army engineers and troops crossing the bridge bore the brunt of German artillery fire. Lieutenant Colonel McClernand Butler, commander of the 3rd Battalion, 395th Infantry Regiment, 99th Infantry Division, recalled: 'I went across the bridge and reported to Major General Louis Craig, commander of the 9th Infantry Division, who had his headquarters in the basement of a hotel. He ordered me to go up and relieve a battalion at Bruchhausen that had been pretty badly shot up. I stayed on that bridge four hours, getting my men across. That was a little hairy because enemy shells were coming in. You could hear them, but we didn't have anywhere to go, so we could only stand there and let them come. Nevertheless, I got my men all the way across.' Private Joseph Rodriguez of the 78th Division recalled, 'They told us to count to 10 and follow the guy before us.'

The initial engineer plan called for three ferry crossings, a treadway bridge and a reinforced pontoon bridge and booms to protect the bridges from German attempts to float mines down the river. Naval Unit No. 1 arrived on 8 March with 24 Landing Craft Vehicle/Personnel (LCVPs) that they had transported from the beaches of Normandy behind the advancing Allied armies and the 86th Engineer Heavy Pontoon Battalion began operating three ferries the following day. On 10 March combat engineer battalions began building a pontoon bridge and a treadway bridge either side of the Ludendorff Bridge. Despite constant artillery fire the engineers completed a 25-ton Class 40 reinforced heavy pontoon p68 ➤

60cm Mörser Karl (Gerät 040/041) heavy siege mortar

Anticipating the need for a weapon to smash the French Maginot Line the German Army ordered the development of a self-propelled 60cm siege mortar in June 1937. The weapon was popularly known as the *Karl* or the *Karlgerät* as artillery General Karl Becker was involved in the development. It was the largest calibre self-propelled gun ever developed. Six production vehicles were delivered from November 1940 to August 1941 and the first four guns were transported to the Russian Front in July 1941.

The *Gerät 040* could fire 3,748lb (1,700kg) *Leichte Betongranate* or 4,742lb (2,151kg) *Schwere Betongranate* (concrete piercing shells) to a range of approximately 4,921.3yds (4,500m). To increase the range the 54cm Gerät *041* barrel was developed that could lob

a 2,755.6lb (1,250kg) shell to approximately 11,373yds (10,400m). The barrels could be interchanged. Using a PzKpfw IV chassis a *Munitionspanzer* was built that could carry four rounds which were loaded by crane. The Gerät could achieve a maximum rate of fire of six rounds per hour.

The 124.4 ton (126,356kg) *Gerät 041* could achieve a road speed of no more than 6.2mph (10 kph). For movement by rail transport the complete *Gerät* was suspended between cantilevered beams on two rail cars. It could also be dismantled into four loads and moved by Culemeyer transporters on roads. In 1945, US forces captured Mörser II with a 60cm barrel and mortar V with a 54cm barrel. A *Gerät 040* is displayed at the Museum of Armoured Forces, Kubinka, Russia.

ABOVE: For transportation the mortar was carried by rail to battlefield locations. *(AN)*

BELOW: The barrel on the Mörser could be changed to fire a 54 or 60cm ammunition round. *(AN)*

ABOVE :
The massive siege mortar was mounted on a purpose-built self-propelled chassis. *(AN)*

RIGHT :
The weapon was supplied with shells from a *Munitons-panzer IV* (a converted tank chassis). This vehicle could carry six rounds of the heavy ammunition. *(AN)*

BELOW: Two of the massive Mörser Karl heavy siege mortars during a training excercise. *(JSS)*

ABOVE: *Nebelwerfer* rockets streak towards the target. *(AN)*

RIGHT: German forces fired *Nebelwerfers*, from mobile units, at US forces around the bridge. *(AN)*

ABOVE: The German army rushed whatever available artillery to Remagen in an attempt to halt the US advance. *(AN)*

RIGHT: Loading the heavy howitzer required a team of five artillerymen. *(AN)*

ABOVE: An Me210, one of which was shot down, during a raid by six aircraft, by D Battery of the 413th Automatic Anti-Aircraft (AAA) Battery. *(PJ)*

LEFT ABOVE: The *Luftwaffe* used many types of aircraft to attack Remagen and the bridge including the He III medium bomber. *(PJ)*

LEFT: A US Army M1 Bofors 90mm mobile anti-aircraft gun. *(JSS)*

'South from Bonn we travelled and stopped at Werthhofen where we waited overnight for priority to cross the bridge. Finally word came and we inched our way along side roads - all roads led to Remagen those few days when a quick end to the war was in balance. Every type of vehicle crowded the roads and the fields were thick with pounding artillery, readied tanks, and ack-ack guns, most of them waiting their chance to get on the small bridgehead. The heavy bombardment of the bridge made crossing very difficult. After hours of short moves and long waits we moved across into the town of Erpel, stopping for a short time to get orders and then on to Unkel. At this time the bridgehead was still very new, and the whole area was still under heavy artillery fire. Momentarily we expected a large-scale counter-attack. Jerry planes of all types made pass after pass at the bridge in effort to halt the troops moving into the bridgehead. We were forced to seek cover even more when our massive antiaircraft barrages went up to knock out these planes. At night the concentrations were so great the sky became as bright as daylight from bursting shells and tracers.' 1st Sergeant Ernie Mettenet of the 99th Infantry Division recalled that 'at times it was actually raining shrapnel from the exploding of

anti-aircraft fire'. The US Army estimated that of the 367 German aircraft which attacked over a nine-day period 109 were shot down by AAA fire and a further 36 were unconfirmed kills. Remagen remains the finest hour in the history of the US Army's AA Command.

Pressured by his staff not to divert resources from Montgomery's Operation 'Plunder' General Eisenhower instructed Bradley to limit the Remagen bridgehead to an area that could be defended by five divisions. Eisenhower cabled the Combined Chiefs: 'Bradley is rushing troops to secure adequate bridgeheads with the idea that this will constitute greatest possible threat as supporting effort for main attack.' Bradley, in turn, instructed Hodges to advance no more than 1,093yds (1,000m) a day, just far enough to prevent the Germans from mining and entrenching around the US force's bridgehead. General Millikin planned to expand the bridgehead in three phases. The first phase line was approximately 2.5 miles (4km) north and south along the river and 1.7 miles (3km) to the east; this ensured the bridge was freed from small arms fire. The second phase line was far enough away to prevent observed artillery fire while the third phase line, which ran north to Bonn then east beyond the autobahn and south to Andernach, ensured the bridge was free of artillery fire.

ABOVE: Panzer-mounted German reinforcements on the move to prevent the Allied forces breakout into the Westerwald. *(JSS)*

LEFT ABOVE: On 8 March seven Ju 87 Stukas and a lone Bf 109 were used in two attacks on the bridge. All were shot down by the joint efforts of many AAA batteries. *(JSS)*

LEFT: A few Me262 jet aircraft were used in lightning attacks against the Ludendorff Bridge, but achieved little success. *(USAF)*

Civilians were evacuated from Remagen to prevent them passing information about the accuracy of German artillery fire and bombing.

By the evening of 9 March the 311th Infantry Regiment had fought through the village of Unkel and pushed beyond the first phase line into the centre of Honnef, 5 miles (8km) north of the bridge. The 311th suffered over 70 casualties during the first 48 hours in the bridgehead. They had also captured 371 prisoners. The next day Shermans and Hellcats provided close support for the 'doughs' who were forced to clear every house in the town. On the right of the perimeter the 310th Infantry Regiment captured the village of Dattenberg, the last high ground to the south which overlooked the bridge. The regiment's 1st Battalion, which bore the brunt of the fighting, lost 60 men casualties but killed 85 Germans and captured another 150. Throughout 11 March the 311th, ably supported by massed US artillery on the west bank, repulsed small, uncoordinated attacks by the 11th Panzer Division. The US units suffered from no shortage of ammunition; the 90th Chemical Mortar Battalion, the first US artillery unit to cross the Rhine, fired over 11,300 rounds between 8 and 25 March. The most difficult challenge for Milliken was extending the bridgehead through the rugged terrain to the east where the US forces were confined to the roads through the villages of Bruchhausen and Ohlenberg. The terrain counter-balanced the Germans' deficiency in numbers and it took more than a week before the US forces could smash through to sever the north-south road between Kretzhaus and Notscheid thus hampering the movement of the German defenders. By that point about 25,000 US troops were concentrated in the bridgehead. General Hodges was dissatisfied with the slow, albeit steady progress, to expand the bridgehead and on 17 March informed Milliken that Major General James Van Fleet would replace him as III Corps commander.

Realising they could not smash through to the Ludendorff Bridge the Germans tried to attack by covert means. Seven naval divers carrying plastic explosives charges tried to enter the Rhine on the night of 16 March but were deterred by US artillery fire. The following night they floated downstream

LEFT: The gun crew of a 240mm M1 Howitzer prepares to fire from a well-camouflaged position. *(JSS)*

RIGHT: One of the seven *Kriegsmarine* (Navy) divers sent to destroy a pontoon bridge with plastic explosive. *(USNa)*

to attack a pontoon bridge. However, US engineers had strung nets across the river to prevent such attacks, riflemen and searchlights, some mounted on tanks, were stationed along the river, and depth charges were dropped periodically. Caught in the glare of the searchlights three of the swimmers were captured while their comrades escaped.

In an act of desperation Hitler ordered V-2 rockets to be used against the bridge. He wanted the bridgehead to be saturated by up to 100 rockets but at this stage of the war such an attack was impossible. From Deventer in the Netherlands *SS Abteilung 500* launched 11 of the rockets against Remagen between 12 and 17 March. Most fell in the Remagen area although one landed near Köln (Cologne) almost 25 miles (40 km) distant. One rocket landed near the Apollinaris Church in Remagen about 1,060yds (1km) from the bridge and another struck the command post of the 1159th Engineer Combat Group killing three and wounding 31. The closest rocket landed at 09.30 on 17 March on a farmhouse on the east bank of the river less than 328yds (300m) from the bridge killing three soldiers billeted in the house. Later that day Hitler sent *SS Abteilung 500* a message of congratulations for destroying the Ludendorf Bridge.

RIGHT: Searchlights were used by US forces to deter enemy attacks on pontoon bridges across the Rhine. *(USNa)*

Cloudpunchers

In 1939 the US Army's mobilisation plan called for an expansion of its force of nine poorly-equipped antiaircraft artillery (AAA) regiments to 46 regiments 30 months after mobilisation was declared. Chief of Staff General George Marshall directed the Army Staff in early 1941 to develop a force of mobile antiaircraft units that could disrupt German *Blitzkrieg* tactics and in May 1942 the War Department raised its objective to more than 600 AAA battalions. This massive force became largely unnecessary after the Allied air forces achieved air superiority over the *Luftwaffe* and many units were converted to artillery units in 1944 or disbanded to provide casualty replacements. Nevertheless, the Anti-Aircraft Command numbered 257,000 men organised into 347 battalions at the beginning of 1945.

Battalions were either gun units equipped with the 90mm M1 AA gun or automatic weapons battalions equipped with a mix of 37mm M1 AA guns, 40mm M1 Bofors guns and quad-mount Browning .50 calibre heavy machine guns. Automatic weapons battalions were equipped either as self-propelled units that could accompany armoured divisions, mobile units to accompany infantry divisions or semi-mobile battalions to protect static locations. Each type of battalion generally had a similar organisation of four firing batteries, a headquarters battery and a support battery. Self-propelled batteries were equipped with eight M15 halftracks armed with a 37mm cannon and twin .50 calibre machine guns and eight M16 halftracks fitted with an M45 Maxson quad .50 calibre mount. Mobile batteries were

ABOVE:
Multiple Gun Motor Carriage M15A1, somewhere in France, late 1944. Note the trailer used to carry extra ammunition and the crews' kit. *(TM)*

ABOVE:
Multiple Gun Motor Carriage (MGMC) M16 with 'in the field' applied winter camouflage, operating in the Bastogne area during late December 1944. *(TM)*

RIGHT:
The crew of a Multiple Gun Motor Carriage M16 ready to engage any aircraft that might appear – note the name ('Hitler's Hearse') painted on the side of the vehicle. *(TM)*

generally equipped with eight towed 37mm or 40mm guns and eight towed M51 quad .50 calibre mounts. The 'Quad .50' was highly successful against aircraft and provided formidable firepower against ground targets; the Brownings could each fire 4-500 rounds per minute to a maximum range of 7,200 yards.

In III Corps the 482nd Automatic Weapons Battalions (Self-Propelled) was assigned to the 9th Armored Division, the 376th AW Battalion was assigned to the 9th Infantry Division and the 552nd AW Battalion to the 78th Infantry Division. Organic to the corps was the 16th AAA Group with two 90mm gun battalions and two AW battalions. Assigned to the First Army was the 49th AAA Brigade with two AAA groups each with one gun and two AW battalions.

Colonel James Madison's 16th AAA Group coordinated the antiaircraft battle at Remagen; as the first AAA headquarters ashore on Omaha Beach the staff had acquired considerable combat experience and Madison was a meticulous planner. In late February 1945 Colonel Charles Patterson, the First Army's AAA staff officer, held a meeting of AAA brigade and group commanders during which tactics were discussed in the unlikely event the army secured a bridge across the Rhine. Patterson decided that protecting the bridge would be the army's AAA priority and directed all units to concentrate at the bridgehead as quickly as possible. Thus on 7 March the III Corps had a formidable force of AAA available to protect the Remagen bridgehead led by experienced, determined commanders who clearly understood what action to take in such a situation.

ABOVE:
A close-up of the front of the quadruple Maxson Mount with the distinctive ammunition boxes. The vehicle is a Multiple Gun Motor Carriage M16. *(JBn)*

RIGHT:
A fully-equipped Half-Track M4A1 81mm Mortar Carrier showing the position of the mortar bomb racks containing the bombs in transport containers. *(TM)*

BELOW:
A Half-Track M4A1 81mm Mortar Carrier in action, Italy 1943. Note the abscence of a .30in M1919A4 machine gun from the skate mount. *(TM)*

The V-2 missile

In 1936 the German Army approved the development of what would become the first ballistic missile to be used in combat. The army hoped to deploy a missile by 1943 capable of delivering a 1 ton (1,016Kg) payload at targets up to 167.8 miles (270km) away. The first test launch of an A-4 at the Peenemünde weapons development centre on 18 March 1942 ended in failure but on 3 October 1942 a test missile flew 118 miles (190km). The weapon became better known by its propaganda name, the *Vergeltungswaffe* (Vengeance Weapon) 2. The V-2 took 5½ minutes to reach its maximum range of 199 miles (320km). Depending on the target that was struck the V-2 typically made a crater 32.8ft (10m) deep and 39-49ft (12-15m) across. The first successful operational mission took place on 8 September when a missile launched from Belgium struck Paris killing six people and injuring 36. In total 3,172 missiles were launched: 1,664 against Belgium, 1,402 against England, 76 against France, 19 against the Netherlands and 11 against the Ludendorff Bridge. The attack on Remagen was one of the few occasions that the V-2 was used against a strictly military target. The missiles aimed at the bridge were launched by the *SS Werfer-Abteilung 500* which was the only unit equipped with a radio guidance system to improve the accuracy of the V-2. These late-production missiles were fitted with the Lorenz *Leitstrahlstellung*, a radio receiver linked to the missile's autopilot system. A radio station on the ground emitted a pair of signals which guided the missile more accurately to the target. According to the US Army the missiles missed the bridge by an average of 1.1 miles (1.7km) in range and 2.2 miles (3.5km) in azimuth.

ABOVE: A V-2 being prepared for launching. *(Ub)*

RIGHT: A V-2 on a launch pad deep in a forest in Holland. *(Ub)*

FAR RIGHT: The V-2 blasts into the sky from a camouflaged launch site. *(Ub)*

BELOW RIGHT: A photograph taken from a Boeing B-17 Flying Fortress of the 101st Bomber Group, 9th US Air Force of a NOBALL Operation against a V-2 launch site in Holland. *(101stbg)*

'I knew instantly that the bridge was collapsing and I turned towards the south bank and ran as fast as I could.'
Lieutenant Colonel Clayton Rust

6

THE BRIDGE COLLAPSES

US Army engineers closed the Ludendorff Bridge on 12 March 1945 and began working round the clock to repair the worst of the damage. Lieutenant Colonel Clayton Rust, commander of the 276th Combat Engineer Battalion and responsible for repair work, estimated the bridge could be reopened on 18 March.

On the afternoon of 17 March Rust was on the middle span of the bridge inspecting progress. 'The first idea I had of any trouble was a sharp report like a rivet head shearing and I noticed a vertical hanger which had been spliced by two turnbuckles was breaking loose and one turnbuckle was dangling, having come loose at the top of the turnbuckle. It appeared as though the bolt holding the turnbuckle to the web of the vertical member had sheared through the web. At that instant I heard another sharp report of a rivet shearing off from my left rear followed by a trembling sensation of the whole deck. Quickly glancing down the deck, the whole deck seemed to be vibrating and dust was coming off the surface. I knew instantly that the bridge was collapsing and I turned towards the south bank and ran

LEFT: US troops inspect damage to the bridge from a German bomb. *(US Army)*

RIGHT: Part of the bridge collapsed at first. Here US personnel search for casualties. *(US Army)*

as fast as I could. While I was running, the east side of the bridge seemed to settle first and I found myself running, in effect 'on a side hill'. The next instant I was engulfed in water. I had no sensation of falling at all.'

Captain Francis Goodwin, of the 1159th Engineer Combat Group, recalled: 'Just prior to crossing the treadway bridge, I heard an unusual sound and looking up saw that the arch of the bridge had just crumbled and the abutment section was settling to the ground. The time was 15.00.' Of the approximately 200 engineers on the bridge at the time 32 were killed and 63 injured.

After the German demolition charge exploded on 7 March the downstream girders were placed under the tremendous strain of supporting the whole weight of the bridge. A III Corps report noted the explosion 'had completely torn apart the lower chord, diagonal, and vertical of the truss at the first panel point south of the north pier. As a result of this, the upstream arch truss had dropped at the north end over one foot below the level of the downstream arch truss at the corresponding point.' The strain was increased as US engineers laid an additional 50 tons (50,802.5kg) of timber decking across the bridge.

RIGHT: Ludendorff Bridge finally collapsed into the Rhine at around 15.00 on 17 March 1945. *(US Army)*

The collapsed Ludendorff Bridge, in the distance are the twin towers of the entrance to Erpeler Ley tunnel. *(Ub)*

BELOW RIGHT: Adolf Hitler Strasse in Remagen was renamed YankeeStrasse by US troops. *(USNa)*

Thousands of men and scores of armoured vehicles and trucks had crossed the bridge in the five days it was open following its capture.

Although only a few German shells struck the superstructure over 600 rounds landed in the vicinity of the bridge as well as a single V-2 rocket which landed 574yds (500m) away. The intense firing of US artillery, 8-inch howitzer batteries alone fired more than 1,000 rounds, created additional shock waves in the vicinity of the bridge. A III Corps report concluded that 'it must be assumed that the bridge collapsed from a combination of causes which, when added together, finally proved the straw to break the camel's back'.

Lieutenant Colonel Edgar Bell, commander of the 90th Chemical Mortar Battalion, noted in his diary: 'The steel bridge over the Rhine at Remagen fell into the river today. It was the most valuable structure ever owned by the US Army. The bridgehead is secure now, but the collapse of THE BRIDGE gave us 'early settlers' a hollow feeling.'

THE FIRST ACROSS THE RHINE
CONSTRUCTED BY
• 291 ENGR C BN
• 988 TDWY CO
• 998 TDWY CO
THE LONGEST TACTICAL BRIDGE BUILT

By the end of March 1945, Allied engineers had assembled over 100 assault bridges across the Rhine. *(US Army)*